What I Can Learn From The Incredible and Fantastic Life of Oprah Winfrey
Published by Moppet Books
Los Angeles, California

ISBN: 978-0-9977145-8-6

Art direction and book design by Melissa Medina
Written by Melissa Medina and Fredrik Colting

Printed in China

www.moppetbookspublishing.com

What I Can Learn From the INCREDIBLE and FANTASTIC Life

— of —

OPRAH WINFREY

By Melissa Medina & Fredrik Colting

Illustrations By Eszter Chen

MOPPET BOOKS

Let's get to know Oprah Winfrey.

She is the most famous talk show host ever. Her show, *The Oprah Winfrey Show*, was the highest-rated TV program of its kind. That means that nobody ever had a more watched talk show, not here, not on Mars, or anywhere else in the Universe! They even call her the "Queen of All Media," which is pretty incredible considering she grew up poor, on a farm, without running water!

The thing people like most about her though is how she has been able to encourage so many people from all over the world to be their best selves.

Oprah's successful TV show made her one of the wealthiest women in history. But more important than the money was that she had the chance to be in front of millions of people on TV every day, and she used that opportunity to bring GOOD into the world.

She had a way of talking to people on her show that made them feel special and cared about. She let people tell their stories, which were often stories that nobody else was telling. Her TV audience felt like she was a friend coming into their homes everyday. And who doesn't like having their friend over!

Many people consider Oprah to be one of the most influential women in the world. In 2013, she even received the Presidential Medal of Freedom from, yep, you guessed it–the President, Barack Obama!

Funtastic Facts

1 She was actually named "Orpah" after someone in the Bible, but people always mispronounced it as "Oprah"—so she changed it to that.

2 She learned how to read when she was only 3 years old.

3 She once gave every person in her audience a new car.

4 She was the voice for Eudora, the mother of Princess Tiana, in Disney's *The Princess and the Frog.*

5 Her company is called Harpo, which is Oprah spelled backwards.

6 Her favorite car is the Volkswagen Beetle. Probably because it's soooo cuuuuuute!

7 Her five dogs give her flowers and personalized cards for every holiday.

8 She was the first black woman in history to become a billionaire!

9 She has given over $400 million to help educate kids, including building schools for girls in South Africa.

10 She has a beautiful estate in California that she calls "The Promised Land".

Let's start from the very beginning...

Oprah was born on a farm in Kosciusko, Mississippi on January 29, 1954. Her childhood was, well, kinda tough.

Her parents, Vernon and Vernita, were young and poor and didn't stay together after Oprah was born. In fact, her mother moved to a big city to find work when Oprah was still just a baby, leaving her to be raised by her grandmother, Hattie Mae, until she was 6 years old.

They lived on a farm without running water and sometimes Oprah had to wear dresses made out of potato sacks because they couldn't afford to buy real ones. But Hattie Mae was a very special lady, and she taught Oprah many things, like how to read when she was just 3 years old, and how to speak up for herself. She gave Oprah a positive sense of herself which she never forgot.

Milwaukee
Wisconsin

When Oprah was 6, she was sent to the big city of Milwaukee to live with her mom again. Hooray! Or so she thought. But life only got worse because they were still poor, Oprah really missed her grandmother, and her mom didn't seem to know quite what to do with her. Oprah felt like she had to take care of herself from a very young age, which made her sad. But luckily, it also made her...

DETERMINED
To Create a Better Life for Herself!

When Oprah got a little older she moved to Nashville, this time to live with her father. He was pretty strict but also pretty smart. He encouraged her to read books every day and to make education her number one goal.

Oprah knew he was right, so she studied hard and became an honors student!

Nashville
Tennessee

Luckily, Oprah loved to read and discovered that she had a real gift for public speaking. In high school, she even won a speech contest which paid for her to go to college.

THE FUTURE WAS STARTING TO LOOK BRIGHTER FOR MISS WINFREY!

In 1971, when Oprah was 17, she entered and won a beauty pageant where she had to speak in front of a big audience.

This really impressed a local radio station, so they offered her a job as a news reader, even though she was still just a teenager.

She immediately loved her new job, and knew that it was the first step

On the Road to Her Career in Public Speaking.

In college, Oprah got a call from the CBS news station in Nashville. They had heard about all her hard work and wanted her to be their news anchor. Now Oprah would be on TV—and she was still only 19 years old.

When Oprah took the job she became both the youngest news anchor and the first African-American female news anchor in Nashville history.

Pretty Impressive, Miss Winfrey!

In 1976, she moved to Baltimore to be an anchor on the WJZ-TV six o'clock news, but she didn't really like it. So her boss said she could try co-hosting a talk show called *People are Talking*. The first day on the job, Oprah knew she had found her calling. She wanted to be a talk show host!

Then in 1983, she was invited to host a morning TV show in Chicago called *A.M. Chicago.* She soon learned that the show wasn't very popular. In fact, it was LAST place in the ratings. But Oprah was so happy to have a job she loved that she decided to give it her all, and in just a few months her show skyrocketed to FIRST place!

It was soon renamed...

THE OPRAH WINFREY SHOW
AND BECAME THE BIGGEST SHOW ON TV!

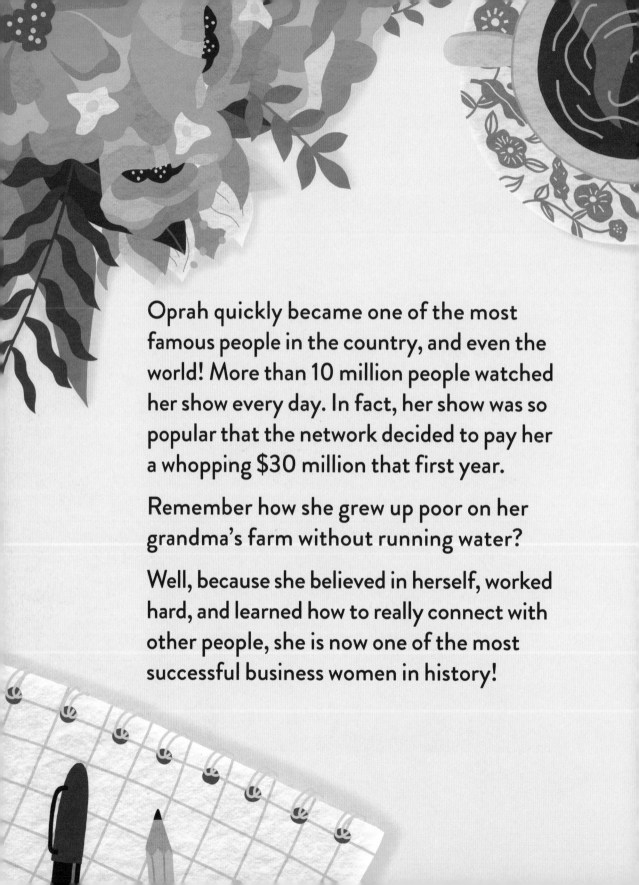

Oprah quickly became one of the most famous people in the country, and even the world! More than 10 million people watched her show every day. In fact, her show was so popular that the network decided to pay her a whopping $30 million that first year.

Remember how she grew up poor on her grandma's farm without running water?

Well, because she believed in herself, worked hard, and learned how to really connect with other people, she is now one of the most successful business women in history!

FOrbes

OPRAH'S
Amazing
LIFE

The First African-American **Woman**
BILLIONAIRE

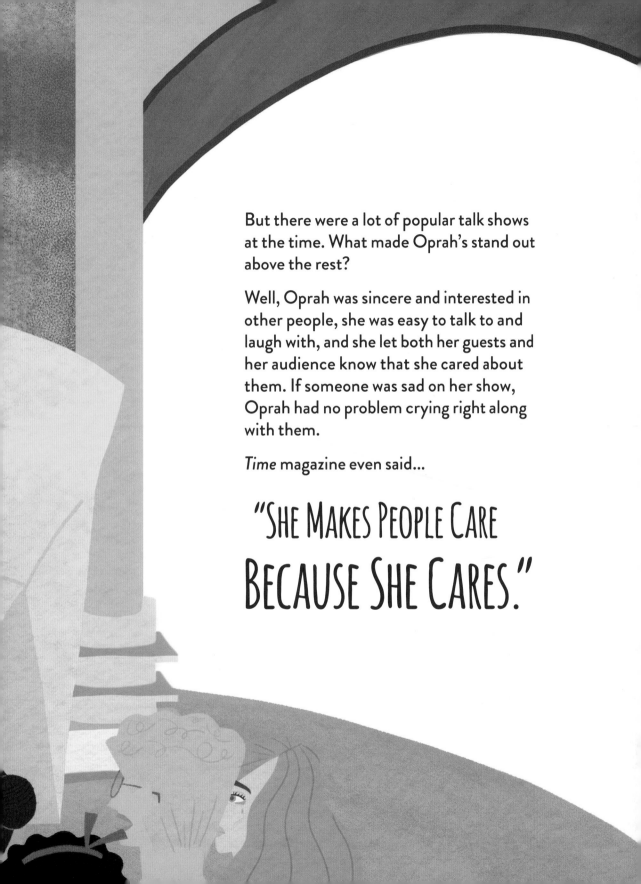

But there were a lot of popular talk shows at the time. What made Oprah's stand out above the rest?

Well, Oprah was sincere and interested in other people, she was easy to talk to and laugh with, and she let both her guests and her audience know that she cared about them. If someone was sad on her show, Oprah had no problem crying right along with them.

Time magazine even said...

"She Makes People Care Because She Cares."

Even though Oprah is most famous for her TV show, she's done a lot of other really cool things too.

She Started a Book Club

Education and reading have always been very important to Oprah, so in 1996, she introduced *Oprah's Book Club* as part of her TV show. And when Oprah recommended a book, it instantly became a bestseller. In fact, they call that "The Oprah Effect".

She Has Her Own Magazine and Radio Channel

She Acts in Movies

She was in a movie called *The Color Purple* in 1985 and did such a great job that she was nominated for an Academy Award!

Then in 2013 she was nominated for more awards for her amazing role in *The Butler.*

Oprah is also very generous, and in 1998 she started a charity called

Oprah's Angel Network

which raised millions of dollars for things like building schools in poor areas and helping families after natural disasters.

She even founded a leadership academy for girls in South Africa because she knows how important a good education is.

THE POSITIVELY POSITIVE LIST

Let's list some positive things about Oprah and her life.

 **1** > ## Oprah Isn't Afraid of Hard Work

She knows that you can be anything you want to be in life, but you also have to work hard to get there. Like when Oprah was a teenager she memorized 20 new words every week. That hard work helped her to be a great TV speaker later in life.

Oprah Is Always Learning < **2**

Oprah loves to learn, and she knows that no matter how old you are, there are always new things to learn and get better at–like how to be healthier or even be a better friend.

♡3 Oprah Helps a Lot of People

Through her show she's helped people that are different feel more understood, helped people with money and supplies when they're down on their luck, and she's always giving people hugs to make them happy when they're sad.

Oprah Looks on the Bright Side 4♡

Even if she has a problem in life, Oprah always tries to focus on all the good things she also has. Remember, there is always something good happening if we just look for it.

How Can I Be Great Like Oprah?

First of all, you should always be yourself because you are already great! But it is a good idea to learn from people that have experience. Here are a few great things we can learn from Oprah.

BE NICE TO PEOPLE!

Oprah often seems to care about people she's just met as much as she cares about her friends. When you are nice to people and show them that you genuinely care about them, they will generally be nice to you too.

READ MORE BOOKS!

Do you want to know what all successful people have in common? They read a lot of books! "Books were my path to personal freedom," Oprah has said. It's not enough to just know *how* to read. You have to make time to read books every day. Your future will thank you!

DON'T GIVE UP!

Even though life was pretty hard for Oprah growing up, she stayed positive and never gave up. If you are positive and remember that things will always get better, then you don't have to be afraid of feeling sad or lonely every now and then.

BIBLIOGRAPHY

Winfrey, Oprah, <u>What I Know for Sure</u>, Flatiron Books, 2014.

McCorvey, J.J., "The Key to Oprah Winfrey's Success: Radical Focus," *Fast Company*, October 12, 2015.

Entrepreneur.com, "Oprah Winfrey," www.entrepreneur.com/article/197558, October 9, 2008.

Academy of Achievement Site, "Oprah Winfrey," www.achievement.org/achiever/oprah-winfrey, Accessed February 15, 2017

Wikipedia.com, "Oprah Winfrey", Accessed February 15, 2017

Biography.com, "Oprah Winfrey Biography.com", www.biography.com/people/oprah-winfrey-9534419, Accessed February 15, 2017

Oprah.com, "Oprah Winfrey's Official Biography," www.oprah.com/pressroom/oprah-winfreys-official-biography, Accessed February 15, 2017